superstars!
superstars!
superstars!

CREATIVE EDUCATION SPORTS SUPERSTARS

jean claude killy

by Charles and Ann Morse

illustrated by
Harold Henriksen

Amecus Street
Mankato, Minnesota 56001

Published by Amecus Street, 123 South Broad Street, P. O. Box 113, Mankato, Minnesota 56001
Copyright © 1974 by Amecus Street. International copyrights reserved in all countries.
No part of this book may be reproduced in any form without written permission from the publisher.
Printed in the United States.
Distributed by Childrens Press, 1224 West Van Buren Street, Chicago, Illinois 60607
Library of Congress Numbers: 74-4489 ISBN: 0-87191-343-7
Cover: Sports Illustrated photo by Eric Schweikardt © Time, Inc.

Library of Congress Cataloging in Publication Data
Morse, Charles.   Jean-Claude Killy.
(Superstars)
SUMMARY: Brief biography emphasizing the career of the French skier
who won three gold medals at the 1968 Olympics.
1. Killy, Jean-Claude — Juvenile Literature.   2. Skis and Skiing — Juvenile literature.
(1. Killy, Jean-Claude.   2. Skis and Skiing — Biography)
I. Morse, Ann, joint author.   II. Henriksen, Harold, illus.   III. Title.
GV854.2.K5M67   796.9'3'0924 (B) (92) 74-4489   ISBN 0-87191-343-7

jean-claude killy

His muscles tensed, Jean-Claude Killy waits. The iron starting gate opens, and the confident Killy bursts down the slope.

Killy takes the starting jump, squaring his shoulders with his skis. His 6-foot frame twists and turns, making a Z at each gate. Out of the corner of his eye Jean-Claude Killy sees he's ahead. Straight over the finish line, Killy raises his poles high into the air.

At Mount Snow, Vermont, Killy had won his first race in the 1972-1973 Benson & Hedges Grand Prix. It was his first victory after "retiring" nearly 5 years before.

For a moment, Jean-Claude could not express what he felt. It was the biggest moment of his life. Like the 2 World Cups, but more, it was a complete comeback. To Killy, it was an "inside explosion."

The moment of victory passed. Jean-Claude Killy went back to the slopes and to his bicycle to train for the next race on the tour.

There's no one secret to Killy's success. When

asked how he does it, Killy simply says that he does what he has to do. Killy is both relaxed and disciplined. He plans every detail, yet skis by instinct. Jean-Claude Killy is a natural athlete who says that he didn't choose skiing. Skiing chose him.

Ski racing was a way of life in Val d'Isere, the mountain town west of Grenoble, France, where Jean-Claude grew up. He was born in Saint-Cloud, a small town west of Paris. In 1946, when Jean-Claude was 3, his family moved to Val d'Isere, or Val as it's called. There his father, Robert Killy, managed a ski shop.

Robert Killy had been an excellent ski jumper and a good Alpine skier. But he had given it up after breaking his leg in an accident. Along with the ski shop, Robert Killy opened a restaurant. Later he bought a hotel. Now he has 2 hotels and 2 ski shops.

Jean-Claude enjoyed his new home. He remembers how some of the roofs sloped to the ground. In winter, drifting snow covered one of the roofs from the peak to the ground. This made a perfect beginner's slope for the 3-year-old Jean-Claude.

"Toutoune" (TooTOON, meaning crazy dog), as Jean-Claude's family called him, played around on

borrowed skis until he was 5. Then his parents gave him his own skis. Jean-Claude and his friends would always make one or two runs down the hills of Val every day after school.

In 1949, when Jean-Claude was nearly 6, his parents were divorced. His sister, France, went to live with their grandparents. Jean-Claude and his younger brother, Michael, lived with their father.

Very early in his life, Jean-Claude had to be responsible for many things at home. Mr. Killy always taught Jean-Claude to work for what he wanted.. The boy often felt this was why he seemed older than other kids his age.

As a 9-year-old, Jean-Claude was quite small for his age. Robert Killy felt that his son was using up all his energy skiing; he had nothing left to make him grow tall and strong. Still, Jean-Claude kept skiing at least 12 long runs every day.

The boy's first victory came in a slalom race when he was 8. Two years later, Jean-Claude won all 3 Alpine events in a youth championship meet, beating even 12 and 13 year olds. As Jean-Claude saw his name appear in newspapers, he realized how much he liked to compete and succeed.

Along with his competitive spirit, Jean-Claude had the ability to imitate the styles of the champion French skiers. This helped him a great deal, for he never had a lesson in his life.

By experimenting with various techniques, Jean-Claude gradually developed a sense of what he wanted to do on skis. He worked hard at his "best-of-everything" style, a style which later brought great success.

There were only 2 years in Killy's early life when he lost out on skiing. A severe lung infection sent the 11-year-old Killy to a boarding school miles away from the people and mountains he loved.

After those 2 difficult years, Jean-Claude was back on skis. At 13, he trained with the French B Team and was invited to compete with the team in the Ilio Colli Cup in Italy. Jean-Claude, knowing that he would not be able to get permission from school to go, went anyway. He ended that trip with a broken leg and a dismissal from school.

The world seemed to stop for Jean-Claude. But when he got out of bed after a few months, he found a strange thing had happened. He had grown 6 inches! Maybe his father had been right. Perhaps Jean-Claude had been too active in his growing years. Lying in bed, he had grown. Now Jean-Claude felt he had the size and strength to become a champion.

Soon Jean-Claude was racing again. He won the 3 main events in the 1959 French junior championships and was being considered for the French national ski team.

The following winter, when Jean-Claude was 15, he made the national team. He traveled and skied with France's best—Adrein Duvillard, Guy Perillat, Michel Arpin. Jean-Claude listened, watched, and learned from them all.

At 16, Jean-Claude dropped out of school, a common practice for members of the French ski team. Later Killy wished he could have had more education. However, travel and experience have made him an educated and cultured man.

Killy skied with plenty of drive and spontaneity when he was 17. He always had the uncanny ability to find the fastest line down a course. He had great speed, but little precision and control. However, he still had time to work on these things.

Jean-Claude began the 1961-1962 season with great confidence. He needed it when he was seeded number 39 for the great slalom race in Val d'Isere.

There are 3 events in international downhill or Alpine ski racing—the downhill, the slalom, and the giant slalom.

The downhill is a fairly straight course and the fastest event. There are checkpoints on the run to assure that each skier stays on course. The slalom is a zigzagging course with a series of "gates" placed quite close to each other. The skier must continually weave from gate to gate. The giant slalom is a combination of downhill and slalom racing. The course is usually longer than a slalom. There are fewer gates and they are spaced farther apart than in a slalom. Downhill racing is usually a single run down the slope. Slalom is always 2 runs with the combined times determining the winner. Giant slalom can also be 2 runs.

In amateur skiing, such as the World Cup events,

there is no head-to-head competition. Each skier goes against the course, and his time determines success. The professional tour in the United States pits skiers against each other in an actual race.

Skiers are ranked by ability, and the best get the lowest numbers and ski first on the initial slalom run. After the course gets chewed up, rutted out, and iced over from the activity of those who ski first, it is very difficult for later skiers to achieve winning times.

At Val d'Isere, Jean-Claude would be the 39th skier on the first slalom run, a very unfavorable.position. But Jean-Claude put it all together. He amazed those present by winning the slalom over Adrein Duvillard and Michel Arpin by more than a second.

After that victory, the newspapers looked toward Killy as the future French ski champion. That victory

brought more than fame to Jean-Claude. Robert Killy then rewarded his son with the chronometer he had used as a pilot in World War II. The chronometer, an instrument that precisely measures time, was a treasure Jean-Claude had always hoped to earn.

Jean-Claude soon learned that he could not rest long after a victory. There was always a new race coming up. The World Championship at Chamonix, France, was to be held soon, and Jean-Claude hoped to be chosen for the French team. Before this event, Jean-Claude pushed too hard for speed during a slalom race in Italy and again broke his leg.

Discouraged, Killy enlisted in the army and spent 6 months in the mountains of Algeria. He got an early leave from the army because he had come down with jaundice. His illness took the punch out of his skiing. Killy struggled to qualify for the 1964 Olympics at Innsbruck, Austria.

Technically, Jean-Claude was prepared for the Olympics. But he had no winning attitude. His health was poor. He was also careless at Innsbruck about waxing his skis properly. His best showing was a fifth in the giant slalom.

Things improved the following season. Jean-

Claude's health was better; and his former teammate, Michel Arpin, offered to handle Killy's equipment. Michel, a good skier, knew everything about ski equipment.

An automobile accident had ended Arpin's racing career. He now worked as technical advisor at a ski factory. He was also able to spend a great deal of time analyzing the many facets involved in Jean-Claude's skiing.

The two Frenchmen worked well together. Michel helped Jean-Claude prepare for races. After a race, the 2 men relaxed together. Michel and Jean-Claude are still good friends today.

Killy had several second place finishes early in 1964-1965 season. Though it was a good beginning, second wasn't good enough for Jean-Claude.

The annual Hahnenkamm race at Kitzbuhel, Austria, is the most demanding downhill race in Europe. The Hahnenkamm is made up of bumps, schusses (or straightaways) and sharp turns. At some point along the way, the skier goes from sunlight to shade within seconds. If the skier hesitates, he's lost.

The slalom at Hahnenkamm was to give proof that Killy was a world class skier. Karl Schranz, the famous Austrian skier, won the first run in the slalom race. But Killy, seeing Schranz's nervousness, came to the start confident. It was here that Killy said he found his own style. Instead of thinking about the next gate, he focused his attention several gates ahead. That gave him time to plan for upcoming difficulties. It also improved his concentration. Alpine skiers say concentration is what determines winners when the world's best racers compete. They all have great reflexes and excellent technique. Most races are decided by fractions of a second. Total concentration makes the difference.

Killy finished the course an amazing 3 seconds ahead of Schranz. The Austrians, who usually save their applause for their own countrymen, cheered wildly for Killy.

When the ski season ended in 1965, Jean-Claude worked hard to improve his English. He knew that it was easy for an athlete, especially a skier, to become shut off from life. He didn't want that to happen. Neither did Jean-Claude want to become too dependent on the French racing system.

The summer of 1966 brought Jean-Claude to the biggest competition he had ever entered: The Federation Internationale de Ski — (International Ski

Federation) — World Championship at Portillo, Chile.

Michel was along with Jean-Claude to make sure the equipment was perfect. Killy chose the fastest run on the course for the downhill race. His style was smooth right to the finish. Even before all the skiers had come down, Michel knew that Jean-Claude had won the title, becoming the best Alpine skier in the world.

Killy would have his chance in 1967 to prove that his win at Portillo was no fluke. It was then that the Evian World Cup was established. Seventeen major races were set aside as World Cup competitions. There were specified points for winning in the downhill, the slalom, and the giant slalom races.

Jean-Claude started the season with 4 firsts in giant slalom competition. Even the Austrian reporters didn't want to say that Killy could beat Austrian skiers in downhill racing. But in the 1967 Hahnenkamm downhill, Jean-Claude set a record. He skied the 2-mile mountain in 2 minutes, 12 seconds.

Killy won the first World Cup. He had 12 firsts, a second, a third, a fourth, and only one no-finish in the 16 races he entered. Jean-Claude won the World Cup with 225 points. No one has yet topped that point total.

Jean-Claude returned home in the late spring of 1967. He relaxed with some auto racing. He also kept in condition by riding his bicycle up and down a steep pass outside Val d'Isere. Killy feels that going downhill fast on a bike is similar to skiing downhill. Both require steady nerves and great confidence.

That summer Michel Arpin had Jean-Claude try several different skis—skis for hard snow and ice, skis for soft snow, skis for everything that could possibly happen at Grenoble, the site of the 1968 Winter Olympics. Michel clocked Jean-Claude on the many different skis as he worked out high in the mountains during July. Finally, they both chose 10 pairs of skis; and Michel went back to the factory to make even better ones.

With the success Killy had enjoyed in 1967, he was the favorite going into the 1968 Olympics. Since Grenoble is close to Val d'Isere, Killy was also the local favorite. All of Jean-Claude's relatives and friends were there holding big signs, "Killy Freres," meaning Killy brothers. General de Gaulle was there. The whole French nation was looking for Killy to win.

On the day of the downhill race at Grenoble, Jean-Claude made a mistake. He usually skis a mile to

see if the wax is adjusted to the snow conditions. But winds had blown the snow away, leaving only icy slopes. Almost all his wax had been rubbed off. When Jean-Claude got back to the starting hut, there was no time to rewax his skis. Michel encouraged Jean-Claude saying he didn't need the wax on that slope. Jean-Claude believed him and won by eight-tenths of a second.

In the giant slalom race, Jean-Claude broke 2 buckles on his boot at the starting gate; he kept on skiing, finishing one and two-tenths seconds ahead of the field. In the second run, an American, Billy Kidd, beat Killy. But for the 2 runs, Killy had won by over 2 seconds.

With 2 gold medals, Jean-Claude went on to the final race, the slalom. Though confident, Killy knew this race would give him the most trouble. The slalom

is always the most difficult for him.

Killy drew number 15 for the first run. This was not a good position. Luckily, the fog that had been hovering over the area, lifted somewhat by his turn. Skiing through the 63 gates in the first run, Jean-Claude had the best time: a half second ahead of the field.

The second run had 69 gates with very sharp turns between gates 18 and 21. This time Killy was the first down the course. But now the fog had returned, making it difficult for the skiers to see more than one or two gates ahead. This slowed down all the skiers. Yet Killy knew he had recorded a good time on the second run.

Haakon Mjoen of Norway posted a time better than Killy's. But shortly afterward it was announced that Mjoen had missed gates 17 and 18 and had been disqualified.

Then came Karl Schranz, Jean-Claude's biggest threat. But Schranz never appeared at the finish line. Schranz claimed a shadowy figure ahead of him blocked his way and caused him to ski off course. He was granted a rerun and posted a time a fraction of a second faster than Killy's.

Newspaper reporters were asking Killy how he felt about losing that last gold medal. Killy, however, remained confident that he would still win it. The Olympic officials deliberated long over Schranz's interference claim. Finally, they ruled that a policeman had crossed the slalom course while Schranz was skiing, but had not interfered with the Austrian skier. Killy was declared the winner.

Three gold medals! Jean-Claude Killy was the hero of the most exciting day ever in Alpine skiing.

Killy was extremely happy. He had learned to live with all the unanswered questions about why a person wins or loses. There are many factors in skiing—weather, mood, equipment, courses, whether you've had enough rest, what you've eaten. Skiing is not a simple sport.

After the Olympics, it was expected that Killy

would become a professional. Jean-Claude, though, wanted to complete the amateur races on the 1968 schedule and try to win the World Cup again. Suddenly the FIS suspended Killy. A French magazine was said to have paid Jean-Claude $7,000 for exclusive pictures of him wearing his 3 gold medals. Amateurs are not supposed to make money in this way.

Killy denied the charge and came to his own defense. He was honest and direct in stating how amateurs need money in order to ski in all the competitions.

Aside from the official money amateur skiers receive, Killy admitted that many skiers receive prize money from ski equipment manufacturers. Jean-Claude never claimed that these practices were within the rules. He simply stated the situation as it was.

Jean-Claude was reinstated by the FIS and went on to win his second World Cup in 2 years.

As the 1968 season was ending, Jean-Claude's mind was not always on skiing. He was thinking about his future. Having dropped out of school, Jean-Claude knew he wasn't trained for business or a trade, and he wanted to do more than be a ski instructor.

Jean-Claude felt that there was no sense in

keeping up the demanding schedule of a ski-racer; nor did he feel he had to keep winning the same races over and over again.

At this time, Mark McCormick, an American who has helped many sports stars to earn millions of dollars, urged Killy to come to America. Killy wasn't sure he wanted to spend a good deal of time in the United States. Jean-Claude said he was never interested in being very rich. He just wanted enough to live well, have a racing car, and travel.

Finally, Jean-Claude decided to accept McCormick's offer. Once he signed with McCormick, Killy's life changed. He became involved in a wide variety of appearances and product endorsements among other activities.

One of his first projects was a TV series — 13 shows on "The Killy Style." He traveled in Europe, Australia, and New Zealand.

Killy and a friend from the French ski team, Leo LaCroix, felt as though they owned the world on this tour. They had only to do relaxed skiing for the cameras. The Frenchmen could stay out late and not worry about being ready for the next race.

Jean-Claude had more than his share of "racer-

chasers." When he would practice, he'd often spot other skiers hiding behind trees to watch his track. Sometimes reporters even interrupted his concentration during those precious 5 minutes before a race. Always polite, Killy would grant an interview that might last right up to his starting time.

Autograph seekers have always flocked around Jean-Claude to watch his style and grace in skiing. They were also attracted by his handsome, winning smile. Since he was an attractive public figure, Killy's relationships with women were often talked about in newspapers and magazines.

Jean-Claude has said that he had no interest in developing a close relationship with any woman. This, he felt, was partly due to his feelings about his mother's leaving their family when he was very young. When Robert Killy remarried, many of Jean-Claude's attitudes changed. He greatly respects his stepmother, Renee. But the biggest change in Jean-Claude's attitude toward women came when he met Daniele Gaubert, a French actress.

Daniele enjoys many of the things Jean-Claude likes. She enjoys sports and has learned to ski well. She was a big help to Jean-Claude when they were both making the movie, "Snow Job." Their relationship deepened over the years, and in November 1973 Jean-Claude and Daniele were married.

Though Killy had had many movie offers, he feels that he is not an actor. He has not made another film since "Snow Job," but he says he would consider it again if the script were right.

The years following Jean-Claude's performance at the 1968 Olympics were fruitful and rewarding ones. Still, Jean-Claude was aware that something was missing. For a long time he wondered if he should seriously get into auto racing. But he felt that he was too old to start over in another sport.

Jean-Claude was facing something common to many athletes. He had to find something new which would involve him as fully as competitive skiing had. It was Jean-Claude's friend, Michel Arpin, who finally convinced Killy to think about skiing again.

In 1972 Jean-Claude decided to make a comeback. A physical education professor helped Killy work out a careful program of running, bicycling, weightlifting, and stretching exercises. The 29-year-old ski-racer started his training for the pro ski tour in July. The first race on the 1972-1973 Benson & Hedges Grand

Prix tour was November 24, 1972, in Aspen, Colorado.

Jean-Claude had a long way to go in a short time. Killy worked out every day and in October began watching for snow reports so he could start skiing.

Killy and Michel were having difficulty finding the right equipment. By the time of the Aspen race, Jean-Claude had spent only 8 days actually skiing.

At Aspen, Jean-Claude was there with boots and skis he knew weren't right. He didn't have a winning spirit. He barely made it into the opening round.

By the next race in Vail, Colorado, Jean-Claude had regained his will to win; but he was still having trouble with his equipment. He had a second and a fourth worth 30 points in the 2 days at Vail. It was a disappointment for Killy, but not for Michel. Jean-Claude's friend saw that the famous skier had recaptured his old drive.

There was a month before the next race. Jean-Claude used each day of it to train. At Mount Snow, Vermont, a happy Jean-Claude Killy won the giant slalom, his first win as a professional.

Jean-Claude placed in the next 4 races, gaining points and money. But it wasn't until the 8th race of the tour at Boyne Mountain, Michigan, that Killy took the lead on the tour. After the Michigan race, he was tied with Colorado's Spider Sabich in points and was ahead of Sabich in earnings.

Killy kept his lead through the next 3 races. By the 12th and final race at Aspen, he had a 30-point lead over Sabich. Killy's best event has always been the giant slalom. But at this race, Jean-Claude lost control on the last bump, missed a gate, and was disqualified. Harald Stuefer, the Austrian pro, placed first in the giant slalom which left him trailing Killy by only 13 points.

The next day's slalom race was the most important event of the Benson & Hedges Grand Prix. Robert Killy was there to watch his son perform. The odds were against Jean-Claude because he hadn't won any slalom races on the tour.

Grand Prix competition is man-against-man, dual-challenge racing. The former U.S. Olympic Coach, Bob Beattie, created this format in 1970 for the pro tour. In the first run, Jean-Claude raced against the little French skier, Alain Penz. At one point Penz was nearly 2 gates ahead and Killy could not overtake Penz. Jean-Claude got up a good rhythm in the second run and kept it all the way down the course. He finished almost nine-tenths of a second ahead of Penz. Killy's win put him in the semifinals of the Aspen slalom.

Killy knew that if Stuefer won, the Austrian would capture the Grand Prix title by 2 points. However, Stuefer lost to America's Tyler Palmer in his second run. Stuefer was out, and Jean-Claude Killy was the Grand Prix champion.

But the Aspen race was not yet decided. Killy faced Palmer in the semifinals. Palmer won the first run, but Killy beat him in the second run by enough of a margin to put Jean-Claude in the finals. Killy outraced the Norwegian, Lasse Hamre, to win the slalom.

Michel, Daniele, and Robert Killy were all overjoyed at Jean-Claude's victories. The Grand Prix championship earned Jean-Claude $40,000. He had also won $28,625 on the tour. Jean-Claude had proved he could indeed come back.

The comeback proved many things about Jean-Claude Killy. At 30, he was still the world's fastest skier. He had matured during retirement. He had adapted to the more exacting pressures of pro racing. He was the leading money winner in the pro tour. Jean-Claude Killy is still a champion.

JACK NICKLAUS
BILL RUSSELL
MARK SPITZ
VINCE LOMBARDI
BILLIE JEAN KING
ROBERTO CLEMENTE
JOE NAMATH
BOBBY HULL
HANK AARON
JERRY WEST
TOM SEAVER
JACKIE ROBINSON
MUHAMMAD ALI
O. J. SIMPSON
JOHNNY BENCH
WILT CHAMBERLAIN
ARNOLD PALMER
A. J. FOYT
JOHNNY UNITAS
GORDIE HOWE

superstars!
superstars!
superstars!

CREATIVE EDUCATION SPORTS SUPERSTARS

WALT FRAZIER
PHIL AND TONY ESPOSITO
BOB GRIESE
FRANK ROBINSON
PANCHO GONZALES
LEE TREVINO
KAREEM ABDUL JABBAR
JEAN CLAUDE KILLY
EVONNE GOOLAGONG
ARTHUR ASHE
SECRETARIAT
ROGER STAUBACK
FRAN TARKENTON
BOBBY ORR
LARRY CSONKA
BILL WALTON
ALAN PAGE
PEGGY FLEMING
OLGA KORBUT
DON SCHULA
MICKEY MANTLE